RELIGIONS OF THE WORLD

I Am
Bahá'í

❧ ANA SAGE ❧

The Rosen Publishing Group's

PowerKids Press™

New York

Published in 1999 by The Rosen Publishing Group, Inc.
29 East 21st Street, New York, NY 10010

First Edition

Book Design: Erin McKenna and Kim Sonsky

Photo Credits: p. 4 © Dusty Willison/International Stock; p. 7 © Johan Elbers/International Stock; p. 8 Skjold Photographs; pp. 11, 20 © George Ancona/International Stock; p. 12 © Peter Langone/International Stock; p. 15 © Bouhafa/International Stock; p. 16 © Erich Lessing/Art Resource; p. 19 © Mimi Cotter/International Stock.

Sage, Ana.
    I am Bahá'í /by Ana Sage.
        p.   cm. — (Religions of the world)
    Includes index.
    Summary: Mona, a member of the Bahá'í Faith, describes her religion's history, practices, and beliefs.
    ISBN 0-8239-5262-2
    1. Bahai Faith—Juvenile literature. [1. Bahai Faith.]
  I. Title. II. Series: Religions of the world (Rosen Publishing Group)
BP365.S29 1998
297'.3—dc21
                                                          98-4190
                                                             CIP
                                                             AC

Manufactured in the United States of America

Contents

1   Mona   5

2   The Báb   6

3   Bahá'u'lláh   9

4   The Unity of the World   10

5   Everybody's Equal   13

6   Prayer   14

7   Bahjí   17

8   The Bahá'í Calendar   18

9   Service   21

10   One Big Family   22

    Glossary   23

    Index   24

Mona

Hi! My name is Mona. My family belongs to a religion called the **Bahá'í Faith** (buh-HY FAYTH). People who follow our religion are called **Bahá'ís** (buh-HYZ). The Bahá'í Faith began about a hundred years ago in a Middle Eastern country called **Persia** (PER-zhuh). Today Persia is called Iran.

Bahá'ís live all over the world. My dad was born in Iran, my mom was born in Mexico, and I was born in Chicago!

◀ People who practice the Bahá'í Faith are all different ages and live around the world.

The Báb

In the mid-1800s, almost everyone in Persia believed in a religion called Islam. But a man who called himself the Báb had some different ideas. Báb means door, or gate, in Arabic, which was the language spoken in Persia. The Báb started a new faith according to his beliefs. He kept some Islamic laws but changed many others. This angered the powerful people in his country, but he didn't care. The Báb told anyone who would listen that soon they would hear the words of God through a very special person.

The word "Báb" means "door," or "gate." Báb may be seen as the door through which Bahá'ís are "led" to their faith. ▶

Bahá'u'lláh

The special person that the Báb was talking about is known today as **Bahá'u'lláh** (bah-hah-oo-LAH). Bahá'u'lláh was born in 1817 to wealthy parents. He could have lived the life of a rich man. But he believed in the ideas of the Báb and even went to jail for them. While in jail, he thought he heard God speak to him. Bahá'u'lláh felt it was his job to become God's **messenger** (MES-en-jer). He started the Bahá'í Faith by spreading God's messages in hundreds of books and prayers.

◀ You can share and learn about the words of Bahá'u'lláh by reading his message with your family.

The Unity of the World

Unity (YOO-nih-tee) means being together. One of the most important things Bahá'u'lláh said was that the world should be united as one family. Bahá'ís don't believe any one person is better than anyone else. We believe that one day everyone on the planet will be equal, and there won't be any war between countries. We believe that everybody will speak the same language, and work to help one another.

By accepting the idea of unity, you learn more about others and make new and interesting friends. ▶

Everybody's Equal

Bahá'ís believe that everyone should be treated fairly and with respect. This includes girls and boys, people with different skin color, and people from every country. This also includes people of other religions. Bahá'ís don't think that just Bahá'u'lláh spoke to God. We believe that Jesus, Moses, Buddha, and other messengers from different religions spoke to God too. Their words are also important to us.

Through the Bahá'í Faith we are all seen as equal, even if we may look different.

Prayer

Prayer is a big part of Bahá'í life. We don't have **traditional** (truh-DIH-shuh-nul) services in a church or temple, like people in other religions. Instead, we pray every day at home. Grown-ups have certain prayers that are said in a special way. Kids can choose from the prayers written in Bahá'u'lláh's books and find a quiet place to say them. When we pray, we face east, which is the direction of a Middle Eastern country called Israel. Israel is a holy land.

The Bahá'í Faith is based on the Islam faith. Both Bahá'ís and Muslims pray daily while facing the holy land. ▶

Bahjí

The holiest spot in the world for Bahá'ís is called Bahjí. Bahjí is in Israel. This is where Bahá'u'lláh was buried after he died in 1892. Thousands of Bahá'ís visit Israel every year to see the mansion, gardens, and small house that are all part of Bahjí. The mansion is where Bahá'u'lláh lived during the last years of his life. But the small house next door is where he's buried. This is a very **sacred** (SAY-kred) place for Bahá'í visitors.

◀ Israel is a holy land for many religions, including the Bahá'í Faith.

The Bahá'í Calendar

Bahá'ís use a different calendar than most people. Our calendar has nineteen months which are each divided into nineteen days. These months have names like Beauty and Perfection. On the first day of every month we celebrate the Nineteen Day Feast. It's not really a feast, though. The Nineteen Day Feast is a day for all the Bahá'ís in one area or neighborhood to pray together and talk about things that are important to us.

The Nineteen Day Feast is about spending time with people we care about. ▶

Service

One of the things we always talk about at our Nineteen Day Feasts is **service** (SER-viss). Service is something you do for other people. My parents say the way to make the world better is to help other kids and grown-ups who aren't as lucky as we are. Every week my sister and I put part of our **allowance** (uh-LOW-ints) into a jar. At the end of the year we send the money to a town in India. The money helps a school where the kids don't have enough clothes and food. My brother actually went to India last year to help build that school.

◄ The act of service can help kids your age in other countries.

One Big Family

A lot of people don't know about the Bahá'í Faith, but there are millions of Bahá'ís around the world. My parents promise that when I'm older they'll take me to meet some of them. They say it's important to know how kids live in different parts of the world. Bahá'u'lláh wrote that no matter how different we are, everyone in the world is part of one big family.

Glossary

allowance (uh-LOW-ints) A certain amount of money given regularly to someone.

Bahá'í (buh-HY) A person who follows the Bahá'í Faith.

Bahá'í Faith (buh-HY FAYTH) A religion that was founded in the 1800s in Persia by a man named Bahá'u'lláh.

Bahá'u'lláh (bah-hah-oo-LAH) The messenger of God for the Bahá'í Faith.

messenger (MES-en-jer) A person who carries a message.

Persia (PER-zhuh) A Middle Eastern country that is now called Iran.

sacred (SAY-kred) Something that is highly respected and considered very holy.

service (SER-viss) Something you do for another person.

traditional (truh-DIH-shuh-nul) Passing something down from one generation to the next.

unity (YOO-nih-tee) Togetherness.

Index

A
allowance, 21

B
Báb, 6, 9
Bahá'í Faith, 5, 9,
    14, 22
Bahá'ís, 5, 10,
    13, 17, 18,
    22
Bahá'u'lláh, 9,
    10, 13, 14,
    17, 22
Bahjí, 17
Buddha, 13

C
calendar, 18

G
God, 6, 9, 13

I
Islam, 6

J
Jesus, 13

M
messenger, 9, 13
Moses, 13

N
Nineteen Day
    Feast, 18, 21

P
prayer, 14

S
sacred, 17
service, 21

T
traditional, 14

U
unity, 10